797.122

1796

Lookout

5-2017

Canoeing

BY MATT DOEDEN

AMICUS HIGH INTEREST • AMICUS INK

Amicus High Interest and Amicus Ink are imprints of Amicus
P.O. Box 1329, Mankato, MN 56002
www.amicuspublishing.us

Library of Congress Cataloging-in-Publication Data
Names: Doeden, Matt.
Title: Canoeing / by Matt Doeden.
Description: Mankato, Minnesota : Amicus High Interest,
  [2017] | Series: Great outdoors | Includes bibliographical
  references, webography and index. | Audience: Grades: K
  to Grade 3._
Identifiers: LCCN 2015023967 (print) | LCCN 2015025517
  (ebook) | ISBN 9781607537977 (library binding) |
  ISBN 9781681510170 (eBook) | ISBN 9781681520766
  (paperback) | ISBN 9781681510170 (pdf)
Subjects: LCSH: Canoes and canoeing–Juvenile literature.
Classification: LCC GV784.3 .D64 2017 (print) | LCC
  GV784.3 (ebook) | DDC 797.122–dc23
LC record available at http://lccn.loc.gov/2015023967

Editor: Wendy Dieker
Series Designer: Kathleen Petelinsek
Book Designer: Tracy Myers
Photo Researcher: Derek Brown

Photo Credits: Tom Stewart/CORBIS cover; Cusp/Superstock
5; Smith Collection/Getty 6; 68/Ocean/Corbis 9; Jason
Lindsey/Alamy 10-11; Zach Holmes/Alamy 13; Michael
DeYoung/Design Pics/Corbis 14; Convery flowers/Alamy
16-17; Jordan Siemens/Getty 18; Minden Pictures/Superstock
21; Design Pics Inc/Alamy 22; Jon Feingersh Photography
Inc./Blend Images/Corbis 24-25; Martin Sundberg/Corbis 26;
Hero Images Inc./Hero Images Inc./Corbis 29

Printed in the United States of America.

HC 10 9 8 7 6 5 4 3 2 1
PB 10 9 8 7 6 5 4 3 2 1

Table of Contents

Let's Go Canoeing

Imagine gliding down a lazy river. Water laps against your canoe. A fish jumps out of the water nearby. You paddle gently through the calm water. An eagle soars overhead. Frogs croak all around you. You take a deep breath. The air is crisp and clean. It's a perfect day for canoeing.

Paddling a canoe through the water is a fun way to enjoy the great outdoors.

This canoe is made of wood.
The paddlers will sit on the
two benches in the boat.

 Q What's the difference between
a canoe and a kayak?

Things You Will Need

You don't need much gear to go canoeing for a few hours. The biggest thing you'll need is a canoe. Canoes are light, narrow boats. Most have one or two seats. Very early canoes were made of wood. Older canoes are made of **aluminum**. But most new canoes are made of plastic or **fiberglass**.

 Canoes and kayaks are alike. In general, canoes are big and open on top. Kayaks are smaller and closed in.

How does a person steer a canoe? **Paddles**. A single-bladed paddle has a short handle and one blade. The flat blade pushes through the water. This moves the boat forward. If you paddle on the right side, it will turn to the left. If you paddle on the left, it will turn right.

 Are there other kinds of paddles?

These canoers use single-bladed paddles. They both paddle on the left to make a right turn.

 Yes! Some canoers use double-bladed paddles. These have a long handle with a blade on each end.

For an afternoon ride, canoers don't need much more than a canoe and a paddle. But long trips mean taking more supplies. Canoers use waterproof bags to carry food and water. They take a rope and an anchor to keep the canoe from floating away. For overnight trips, they bring a tent and a sleeping bag.

A camper loads his canoe.

A canoe trip can be a short one down a river. Or it can be an adventure across several lakes and rivers. Some people travel deep into the wild. They need gear to help them find their way. The most basic gear is a map and **compass**. Some people use **GPS** units. These show them exactly where they are.

These paddlers explore canyons in Utah. Plastic bags and map covers keep their gear dry.

A family keeps safe by wearing life vests. These vests help people float in the water.

 Q How can I keep the boat from tipping over?

Safety First

Canoeing is fun. But it does have some dangers. Canoes can tip over. Riders can fall out. To stay safe, every rider should wear a **floatation device**, or life vest. Each year, about 50 paddlers drown. Many of them do not have on a life vest. Some states have laws about life vests. But even if people aren't required to wear life vests, they should. It's much safer.

 Stay low. When you move in the canoe, stay crouched. Sit in the middle of the canoe. Sitting close to a side can make the boat tip.

Big waves can cause canoes to tip over. Some canoers use **float bags**. These air bags tuck into the front or back of the boat. They help a tipped canoe float. Even if a canoe stays upright, waves can wash water into the boat. Some people bring small buckets. They use them to bail water out of a canoe.

Yellow float bags are tucked in this canoe.

If all is well, you can use a cell phone to take photos. Call for help if things go bad.

 Can I canoe by myself?

No matter where you go, tell someone where you are going. And tell them when you think you'll be back. You'll want emergency gear, too. A cell phone is a good start. You can call for help if you're in trouble. In places with bad cell reception, bring a two-way radio. Leave one with nearby friends or family.

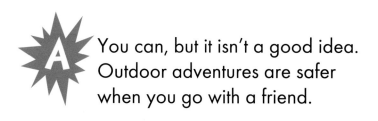
You can, but it isn't a good idea. Outdoor adventures are safer when you go with a friend.

One good way canoers stay safe is by watching the weather. Stay close to shore if storms are in the forecast. High winds and thunderstorms mean danger. Stay off the water if the weather is bad. If you are on a long trip when the weather turns bad, land the canoe and find shelter.

Storm clouds gather over
this lake. Smart paddlers
will stay off the water.

Canoeing in fast water is exciting!

Where to Go

You can canoe almost any place there's open water. Many people relax on lakes. Some enjoy gentle rivers. Some take trips along ocean shores. And others like to take on **rapids**. Pick a spot that fits your skills. Paddling can be dangerous if the water is moving too fast.

Small lakes are a good place to start. They rarely have strong currents or big waves. Stay close to shore. Master basic paddling and turning. Many parks have canoe rentals. Some even offer classes to teach you how to paddle.

A calm lake is a good place to learn how to paddle a canoe.

Paddlers carry canoes from one waterway to the next.

Are canoes heavy? Are they hard to carry?

State and national parks are great for long trips. Parks with lots of waterways are best. Some parks are set up just for canoers. To get from lake to lake, canoers often have to carry their canoes over land. This is called **portaging**. Follow marked portage trails to stay safe and not get lost.

 They can be! Some adults can carry a canoe alone. But lots of people find a partner to help.

Have Fun!

Canoeing takes some planning. With a bit of time, you'll be gliding across the water. It doesn't matter if it's a quick afternoon ride or for a longer overnight trip. It's all about having fun. So load up, grab a paddle, and hit the water!

Some canoers take fishing gear along. They paddle to a good fishing spot.

Glossary

aluminum A strong, lightweight metal.

compass A tool that shows which direction North is to help users find their way.

fiberglass A strong, lightweight material made of woven fibers of glass.

float bag A bag of air that fits inside a canoe to help it float better in case it tips over.

floatation device A piece of safety gear, such as a life vest, that helps a person float in the water.

GPS Short for "global positioning system," GPS units use satellites orbiting Earth to determine a person's location.

paddle A pole with a broad blade at one end or both ends; canoers use paddles to push their boats through the water.

portaging Carrying a canoe over land to get to the next waterway.

rapids Fast moving water that creates rough waves.

Read More

Champion, Neil. *Wild Water: Canoeing and Kayaking*. Mankato, Minn.: Smart Apple Media, 2013.

Mason, Paul. *Kayaking and Canoeing: The World's Best Paddling Locations and Techniques*. Mankato, Minn.: Capstone Press, 2011.

Norris, Ashley P. Watson. *How to Canoe and Kayak Like a Pro*. Berkeley Heights, NJ : Enslow, 2014.

Websites

Canoeing.com
http://www.canoeing.com

Canoeing For Kids
http://www.canoeingforkids.org

Canoe Safety Tips
http://dnr.wi.gov/org/caer/ce/eek/nature/camp/canoesafety.htm

Index

About the Author

Author and editor Matt Doeden has written hundreds of children's and young adult books on many topics. His titles include Junior Library Guild selections and have been listed among the Best Children's Books of the Year by the Children's Book Committee at Bank Street College. Doeden, a recreational canoer, lives on a lake in Minnesota with his wife and two children.